Original title:
Creative Souls

Copyright © 2024 Swan Charm
All rights reserved.

Editor: Jessica Elisabeth Luik
Author: Lan Donne
ISBN HARDBACK: 978-9916-86-272-8
ISBN PAPERBACK: 978-9916-86-273-5

Thought Paint

In the quiet of my mind's estate,
Brushstrokes of dreams softly allay,
Colors merge in fateful spate,
Where shadows dance and light does play.

A canvas vast, emotions spill,
Whispers of gray in twilight's hue,
Memories on edges still,
Past and present blend anew.

Echoes of laughter, tides of sorrow,
Swirling clouds in a dawn-lit sky,
Every shade a stolen morrow,
As time we chase, yet not deny.

Love in reds and fears in blacks,
Pallets of hope, a spectrum vast,
Through the void my heart retracts,
Hope's bright hues in dreams are cast.

In each stroke, reflections rise,
Shadows fade, and truths unfold,
In thought paint, the spirit flies,
As stories in silence, bold.

Timeless Creation

In the stillness of dawn's embrace,
Whispers of existence trace.
Time a canvas, wide and free,
Painting moments endlessly.

Silent fields where dreams reside,
Patterns in the stars confide.
Every breath a brand new start,
Nature's beat an eternal heart.

Waves that echo through the sky,
Stories woven, reason why.
In this fleeting cosmic dance,
Creation fuels every chance.

Symphony of Thought

Waves of wisdom crest and fall,
Ideas whisper through the hall.
Reason twines with dreams aglow,
Symphony of thought in flow.

Riddles turn in minds awake,
Harmonies the quiet make.
Each reflection, note and word,
In the silence ever heard.

Connections weave in unseen strings,
A melody of endless springs.
Within the echoes, truths unfold,
The symphony of thought, untold.

Inspirational Shadows

In shadows cast by evening light,
Dreams awaken, taking flight.
Boundless hope in twilight's grace,
Whispers in the silent space.

Darkened trails that shape the dawn,
Every night to day is drawn.
Shadows tell of paths once crossed,
Guiding those who might be lost.

In their depth, new visions grow,
Seeds of thought in shadowed glow.
Every dusk evokes the spark,
In shadows' play, find the mark.

The Abstract Whisper

Colors blend in twilight's hue,
Forms of thoughts begin anew.
Abstract whispers shape the air,
Creativity laid bare.

Brush of wind, a silent muse,
Compels the mind, thought to fuse.
Every line a whispered prayer,
Abstract dreams beyond compare.

Glimmers in the shadowed mist,
In the unknown, truth exists.
The whisper calls a deeper dive,
Where abstract thoughts come alive.

Brushstrokes of Thought

In twilight's gentle hush,
Ideas softly blend,
Colors weave like dreams,
Imagination's friend.

Canvas of the mind,
Hues both bright and dim,
Whispers form a tapestry,
Of vision's hopeful hymn.

Each stroke tells a tale,
In silence, hopes unfurl,
A symphony of shades,
That paints an inner world.

The Poet's Canvas

A blank slate before me,
Ink's destiny unwinds,
Words like falling stardust,
Glow within my mind.

Every phrase a brushstroke,
Each verse casts a spell,
In this quiet stillness,
Imagination dwells.

This canvas of paper,
Receives thoughts pure and true,
In poetry's embrace,
The soul finds skies anew.

Whispers of Genius

In shadows softly speaking,
Genius breathes its muse,
Whispers in the silence,
Light the paths we choose.

Ideas waltz like phantoms,
In corridors unseen,
Ethereal and fleeting,
Where inspirations glean.

To catch these ghostly murmurs,
One must dare to dream,
For in their quiet whisper,
Lies brilliance' gentle gleam.

Soaring Visions

In skies of dreams, where whispers grow,
Feathers drift in a gentle flow.
The world below is but a scene,
A tapestry of what might've been.

Eyes closed tight, wings spread wide,
We journey far where hopes reside.
From mountain peaks to oceans blue,
A canvas where all thoughts are true.

Sunlight glows in silent mists,
Beyond the reaches of clenched fists.
Every climb, each daring flight,
Reflects the heart's own brilliant light.

Through clouds of gray and azure skies,
The dreams we chase ne'er disguise.
In every whisper, rustle, sigh,
Our soaring visions truly fly.

Illuminated Muse

In shadows dense, a light appears,
A beacon through the tangled years.
She whispers songs of truths disclosed,
In silent nights, her voice composed.

Her radiance cuts through dark and dull,
With words that mend, with hope that pull.
She weaves the stars in every verse,
Unveiling wonders, bright or terse.

Her presence fires the heart's delight,
In every stroke, in every light.
With quill in hand, she paints the sun,
A masterpiece for everyone.

Through whispers soft and echoes pure,
Her guiding light helps dreams endure.
In every glance, a tale ensues,
The glow within, our muse renews.

Dream Chisels

With each keen edge, the dreams are hewn,
In moonlit nights or afternoon.
From marble blocks of fleeting thought,
Our deepest hopes are finely wrought.

In sculptor's hands, the visions form,
Through tempests loud and moments warm.
A stroke, a cut, a delicate touch,
Each whisper speaks, each shadow much.

The dust of doubts falls to the floor,
In shapes that guard the heart's own core.
Emerging clear from foggy mists,
The dream in stone forever persists.

Chiseled paths in hardened clay,
Reveal the souls that find their way.
With every blow, the form refines,
A lasting mark on fleeting times.

Imaginative Winds

Through tempest's gale and gentle breeze,
The winds of mind traverse with ease.
They carry thoughts both wild and free,
From distant lands and starry sea.

In whispering tones or howling cries,
They paint the canvas of the skies.
With every gust, a story told,
Of ancient myths and hearts so bold.

They break the bounds of time and space,
Through open fields, in secret place.
A zephyr's kiss, a storm's embrace,
In every gust, a hidden grace.

The winds of thought will always blow,
Wherever hearts and minds may go.
With every breath, a seed released,
From imaginations, dreams increased.

Mosaic of Daydreams

In the tapestry of thought, I find my way,
Through fields of gold where ideas play.
Each fragment whispers secret schemes,
In the mosaic of daydreams.

Colors blooming in my mind,
A vision that's one of a kind.
Threads of wonder tightly weave,
A world that I can believe.

In this land of endless skies,
Where imagination never dies.
I paint my hopes, my fears, my gleams,
In the mosaic of daydreams.

A sanctuary of the soul,
Where broken pieces make us whole.
Each shard of light forever beams,
In the mosaic of daydreams.

Poetic Brushfires

Words ignite in fervent blaze,
Lighting up the darkest days.
Spoken truths in whispered choirs,
Set aflame like poetic brushfires.

Each verse a spark, each rhyme a glow,
In the twilight, passion shows.
Flickers dance 'midst ink and lyres,
Burning bright in poetic brushfires.

Through rocky paths and silent nights,
Pen and parchment touch new heights.
Paper lanterns, fueled by choirs,
Float above these brushfires.

Embers fade, yet linger on,
In our hearts, they're never gone.
Ashes hold the love-inspires,
From eternal poetic brushfires.

Alchemy of Artistry

From ordinary turns to gold,
With every story ever told.
In hands of those who dare to dream,
Lives the alchemy of artistry.

Dance of colors on a canvas white,
Breath of shadows, kiss of light.
Transforming thoughts to ecstasy,
With the alchemy of artistry.

Chisels shape the formless stone,
Bringing life to the unknown.
Echoes in eternity,
By the alchemy of artistry.

Words and music, painting, clay,
We create, we mold, we play.
Crafting from a wild sea,
An endless alchemy of artistry.

Twilight Compositions

In the silence, dusk unfolds,
Whispers of a story told.
Stars align in soft positions,
Crafting twilight compositions.

Moonlight brushes shadows deep,
Stealing secrets, memories keep.
Nighttime's symphony on missions,
Sings the twilight compositions.

Crickets' chorus hums along,
Adding depth to nature's song.
Every note in sweet transitions,
Art in twilight compositions.

Dreams awoken, slowly glide,
Through the spaces they reside.
Boundless thoughts in grand renditions,
Echo twilight compositions.

Whimsical Notations

On parchment white, the ink will dance,
A symphony of chance and grace.
Notes and curves in rhythmic trance,
Each line a dream, a world to trace.

In quiet realms of twilight dusk,
Where shadows play and spirits roam,
The quill obtains a gentle trust,
To sketch a path through time and home.

A melody of thoughts entwine,
In whimsical and fleeting flight.
Upon each stroke, a hidden sign,
Conveys a whisper in the night.

As stardust brings the evening's hush,
The notes still float on gentle breeze.
Their silent songs, a subtle blush,
In moonlit dreams, the heart at ease.

Eruption of Thoughts

In tempest fields, the mind does spark,
With lightning bolts of fierce decree.
A torrent wild, amidst the dark,
Unfurls the depths of memory.

Like lava flows, each notion stews,
In cauldrons deep, and seething bright.
An inner world, devoid of clues,
Erupting forth from depths of night.

Volcanic storms of fervent dreams,
Burst forth in showers, red and gold.
Thought currents carve their primal streams,
Reshaping lands both hot and cold.

The aftermath, a silent peace,
As ash descends on muted ground.
From chaos, sparks a new release,
A fertile soil, with thoughts unbound.

Drifting in Design

Patterns weave through cosmic threads,
In tapestry of color, bold.
Drifting in design, they spread,
Stories of the young and old.

Each thread a whisper, tale untold,
Of lives entwined in fate's embrace.
A symphony in weave and fold,
Reflecting every time and place.

Stars align in cosmic rhyme,
Eclipsing dreams in silent flight.
Within the fabric, sands of time,
We find our paths, both day and night.

Drifting through the vast unknown,
Our spirits trace the woven line.
In every thread, a seed is sown,
To bloom within design divine.

Whispers Through Clay

Hands entwine in earthy dance,
Molding dreams from primal clay.
In each touch, a heart's romance,
In every form, a voice will stay.

From formless mound to statue grand,
With nimble grace, the fingers ply.
A whisper flows from craftsperson's hand,
In silent song, the spirits sigh.

Textures blend and contours speak,
Of truths from deep within the soul.
Each curve a secret, strong yet meek,
In clay, the stories find their role.

Fired by passion's fiercest flame,
The shapes emerge with fervent glow.
Whispers through clay, though form may wane,
Their essence lingers, hearts to know.

Vision's Pulse

In twilight's gentle, tender grace,
The shadows dance, a soft embrace.
Dreams awaken, rise and sing,
In the heart where hopes take wing.

Colors burst in silent night,
Stars ignite the sky's delight.
Whispers on the breeze do play,
Guiding lost souls on their way.

Eyes that see beyond the mist,
Seek the truth that can't be kissed.
Through the darkness, piercing through,
Vision's pulse, the world anew.

Mysteries unfold, so bright,
In the depths of endless night.
Every whisper, soft and clear,
Tells the tale we long to hear.

Radiant beams embrace the dark,
Leaving in their wake a spark.
And the heart, it beats in time,
To the silent, endless rhyme.

Ethereal Creations

Spirits waltz in twilight's gleam,
Crafting worlds within a dream.
Soft as breath, the moments blend,
Whispers of the souls transcend.

Threads of silver weave the night,
Tales untold of silent flight.
Ethereal, the shadows spin,
Guardians of what's within.

Stars are painted, strokes so fine,
On the canvas, out of time.
Every brush, a story weaves,
In the hush of gathered eves.

Moonlight's fingers gentle trace,
Patterns of a fleeting grace.
Unseen hands that shape the sky,
Fleeting moments drifting by.

Echoes linger, soft and slow,
In the dream where lifetimes flow.
Ethereal creations thrive,
In the art that keeps us alive.

Fables of Palette

Canvas bare, awaits the brush,
Colors speak without the hush.
Fables told through crimson, gold,
Stories new and stories old.

Brushes dance in rhythmic sweep,
Secrets that the pigments keep.
Every stroke, a life unfurled,
In the hues that shape the world.

Tides of emerald, skies of blue,
Art that breathes and speaks to you.
Palettes whisper, tales unfold,
Mysteries in every bold.

Portraits sing of joy and pain,
Through the sunshine and the rain.
In the spectrum, find the truth,
Of innocence and age and youth.

Masterpiece of light and shade,
In the pigments deftly laid.
Fables crafted, pure, sincere,
In the art we hold so dear.

Conductor's Enchantment

Batons rise with silent grace,
Guiding symphonies through space.
Notes cascade through air unseen,
Crafting magic soft, serene.

Melodies entwine, reveal,
Echoes of a soul's appeal.
In the cadence, life takes flight,
In the day and in the night.

Strings and woodwinds intertwine,
Harmony's elusive line.
Every chord, a tender spell,
Words that silent hearts can tell.

Music weaves a timeless thread,
Through the living, through the dead.
Conductor's hand, an artist's art,
Shaping dreams that stir the heart.

Echoes linger, soft and pure,
In the notes that must endure.
Enchantment found in every song,
Where the soul and music belong.

Lyrical Mirage

In the desert of dreams, where shadows play,
Winds whisper secrets at the break of day.
Golden dunes ripple like the sea,
A mirage of thoughts, yearning to be free.

Silent songs fill the arid air,
Whispers of stories, woven with care.
Ephemeral visions, born from the sand,
Fleeting like time, forever unplanned.

Stars sprinkle silver on the midnight sky,
Glimmers of hope in a world gone dry.
Horizons stretch, infinite and wide,
As dreams awaken, with a quiet sigh.

Innovative Echoes

Echoes of brilliance, in the mind's great hall,
Whispers of ideas, awaiting their call.
Through corridors of thought, they twist and wind,
Finding new paths, eager to be kind.

Imagination blooms in the fertile mind,
Seeds of tomorrow, a trail left behind.
Boundless potential in every spark,
A beacon of light in the deepest dark.

From chaos, order, born anew,
Patterns emerging, as dreams pursue.
Innovative echoes, they never fade,
In the heart of creation, they gently wade.

Mind's Eye

Through the mind's eye, a world unfolds,
A tapestry of dreams, in colors bold.
Visions dance on neurons' thread,
Woven with thoughts we've never said.

In shadows' embrace, the light is found,
Silent whispers, a symphonic sound.
Ideas cascade like a waterfall,
Boundless and free, they answer the call.

The mind's eye sees beyond the veil,
A realm where heart and spirit sail.
Infinite landscapes, where dreams reside,
In the mind's eye, we find our guide.

Inspired Brush

With an inspired brush, the canvas wakes,
A symphony of hues, an art it makes.
Each stroke a whisper, a silent plea,
A story unfolds for the world to see.

The colors blend, emotions weave,
In the artist's hand, dreams believe.
Silent musings transform to sight,
A dance of shadows, birthing light.

From the heart to the hand, a journey flows,
In every curve, the passion grows.
An inspired brush paints life's refrain,
A timeless tune, in vibrant gain.

Architect's Internal Symphony

In sketches, whispers of a dream,
Blueprints dance, a tranquil stream.
Angles, arcs in melody
Craft a structure, wild and free.

Echoes of the mind take flight,
Building towers in the night.
Foundations rooted, steadfast ground,
Creativity all around.

Columns rise, a symphony,
Harmony in masonry.
Silent music, crafted beams,
Every detail softly gleams.

Windows framed with light and love,
Visions drawn from skies above.
Spaces formed from heart and soul,
Every piece a vital role.

In every brick, a whispered song,
In every wall, a pulse strong.
Tune of labor, grace in hand,
A symphony to forever stand.

Auras of Craft

Hands that weave with threads of gold,
Crafting stories, tales untold.
Looms that hum a gentle tune,
Fabric dancing, bright as noon.

Tools in hand, they shape and mold,
Bringing warmth to nights so cold.
Silken threads and sturdy yarn,
Craftsmen work from dusk till dawn.

Colors blend in perfect hue,
Every shade a story new.
Patterns trace a history,
Woven with such mastery.

Leather bound with tender care,
Craftsmen's love in every tear.
Carving life from blocks of wood,
Each creation, understood.

In each craft, a soul resides,
Love and skill where art abides.
Auras glowing, hands and heart,
Crafting from the very start.

Galactic Brushstrokes

Stars are sparks on velvet night,
Galaxies in swirling light.
Nebulae in colors vast,
Cosmic art that's made to last.

Planets painted, worlds in spin,
Universe, the canvas thin.
Swirling, twirling through the space,
Brushstrokes delicate, with grace.

Comets streak with tails ablaze,
Dancing through eternal maze.
Spaces filled with whispers strong,
In the void, a silent song.

Milky Way's majestic sprawl,
Galactic wonders, one and all.
In the vast infinity,
Artistic serendipity.

Celestial brush, divinely wield,
Crafting visions unconcealed.
Universe in vibrant hue,
Endless masterpiece in view.

The Weaver's Tale

Threads of story, tales in weave,
Every pattern we conceive.
Ancient lore in yarn is found,
Spinning tales that do astound.

Warp and weft in harmony,
Crafted with such artistry.
Stories told in every thread,
Colors rich, by legends led.

From the loom, a tale unfolds,
History within it holds.
Hands that work with tender grace,
Weaving magic, time and space.

Tapestries, the weaver's dream,
In each stitch, a secret scheme.
Fables, myths in fabric form,
All within, so safe and warm.

Every thread, a life's detail,
Woven in the weaver's tale.
From the past to futures bright,
Stories spinning into light.

Harmony in Color

In hues of dawn and night's embrace,
Colors merge in gentle grace,
A symphony of light and shade,
In nature's art, so richly laid.

Petals blush with morning's kiss,
Blending dreams in fields of bliss,
From golden dawn to twilight's glow,
Harmony's colors in soft flow.

Verdant hills and azure skies,
Nature's palette never lies,
In autumn's fire and winter's gleam,
Color's harmony, a painter's dream.

In melodies of bright and hue,
Tales in every shade we view,
From whispers of the ocean's blue,
To the sun that bids adieu.

Through each season's lovely flight,
Colors weave both day and night,
In silent chords that gently flow,
Harmony in color we forever know.

Canvas of the Heart

Upon the canvas of the heart,
Impressions form, a tender art,
With brushstrokes bold and whispers fine,
In love's true colors, stories line.

Each heartbeat holds a hue so rare,
Moments captured, beyond compare,
In joy's bright yellows, sorrow's gray,
The soul's own artistry in display.

Like rivers flowing through each vein,
Emotions blend, a sweet refrain,
From crimson passion's flowing tide,
To peace in soft pastels that bide.

Colors of trust, of dreams we weave,
In heart's embrace, we truly live,
A masterpiece within our core,
Expansive as an open shore.

In love's deep gallery we stand,
With every beat, with every hand,
Upon this canvas, bright and true,
The heart reveals its every hue.

The Designer's Reverie

In the designer's reverie,
Ideas sprout like blooming trees,
Patterns dance in intricate rhyme,
Crafted through the hands of time.

With needle's thread and pencil's glide,
Visions take their place and bide,
From thought to form in quiet birth,
A realm of beauty finds its worth.

Textures blend and colors meet,
In harmony of the elite,
Shapes emerge in gentle grace,
Filling dreams with vivid space.

Each stitch a whisper, line a song,
In the designer's world, so strong,
Echoes of imagination pure,
Through every creation they endure.

From dawn's first light to twilight's ease,
Every stroke and cut to please,
In this reverie that knows no end,
Design and dreams forever blend.

Ink-spun Fantasies

Ink-spun fantasies take flight,
On parchment pale in soft moonlight,
Words cascade in silent streams,
Weaving through the poet's dreams.

In every line a world unfolds,
Stories of the brave and bold,
Myths and legends intertwine,
In realms where endless stars align.

With quill in hand, the muse does speak,
Of love's profound and sorrow's peak,
Each verse a world within its own,
In ink the seeds of magic sown.

No boundaries hold these flights of mind,
Imagination unconfined,
In tales of wonder, dark and bright,
The mind takes wing, in endless flight.

Through ink's embrace the soul explores,
New vistas, lands, and distant shores,
In every scribe's enchanted gaze,
Ink-spun fantasies forever blaze.

Odyssey of Shapes

In the realm of angles, sharp and bright,
Lines weave stories, left and right.
Circles dance in endless flight,
Geometric dreams, pure delight.

Triangles whisper ancient lore,
Squares stand firm, forever more.
Rectangles stretch from shore to shore,
Shapes of wonder, we explore.

Hexagons form a honeyed maze,
Pentagons in starlit praise.
Octagons in mirrored gaze,
An odyssey in countless ways.

Ellipses curve in silent grace,
Contours trace a seamless face.
Tessellations interlace,
Infinite in bounded space.

In this world of structured lines,
Patterns speak, transcend confines.
Mathematics intertwines,
In shapes, the cosmos shines.

Flame of Craft

Hands that forge with tender might,
In fire's heart, they find their light.
Metal yields to vision's sight,
Crafted dreams from day to night.

Hammer's symphony in sparks,
Anvils hold the ancient marks.
Creation born from ember's arcs,
Ignited souls, ignited hearts.

Wood and steel, a sacred bond,
With each strike, a magic wand.
Artistry in heat beyond,
Craftsmen in devotion, fond.

Chisels carve with patient grace,
Rough forms take a polished face.
In every grain, a silent trace,
Flame of craft, time can't erase.

Through the ages, skill ignite,
Gifting form to human plight.
Craft's true flame, forever bright,
In each piece, a timeless sight.

Eternal Drafts

Scrolls of thought, where ink may dwell,
Pages whisper tales to tell.
In margins wide, ideas swell,
Eternal drafts in mystic spell.

Quills may glide on parchment's skin,
Tracing words that lie within.
Stories born, yet to begin,
Whispers of the heart's own kin.

Fragments of a soul afloat,
In each line, a secret note.
Unfinished verses gaily float,
Through time and space, they gloat.

Bound in leather, cracked with age,
Scripts of wisdom, poet's wage.
On every line, life's hidden stage,
In drafts, our legacies engage.

Endless drafts in boundless flight,
Ink-stained hours in the night.
Thoughts take wing in starlit light,
Eternal drafts, a writer's rite.

Potter's Silent Echo

Clay upon a wheel does spin,
Potter's hands, it flows within.
Form is found where dreams begin,
Silent echo, kiln's quiet kin.

Mud transformed to shapes anew,
Simple earth in craft's debut.
Fingers guide, intentions true,
Silent songs in every hue.

Kiln that breathes a fiery breath,
Births each piece in life and death.
Potter whispers, warm caress,
Silent echoes none suppress.

From the earth, creation's might,
From the void, a form of light.
In each groove, a whispered sight,
Silent echo's pure delight.

Patterns, glazes, colors blend,
Journeys told from end to end.
Potter's touch in curves extend,
Silent echoes that transcend.

Verse of Dreams

A whisper in the midnight air,
A secret only moonlight shares,
Softly woven, a dreamer's snare,
Hushed voices in the night's fair pairs.

Stars above, they gently gleam,
Threads of silver in a seamless stream,
Crafting visions from our deepest theme,
In the serene realm where we weave our dream.

The sands of time, silently flow,
The gentle river, where dreams grow,
A tapestry of night, aglow,
Guiding hearts to where they must go.

In slumber's hold, we freely soar,
Beyond the threshold of night's door,
In the dreamscape, forevermore,
We find the secrets we adore.

Awake, the dawn will softly call,
Dreams dissolve like snowflakes fall,
Yet in our souls, they stand tall,
A gentle whisper we recall.

Architects of Thought

In the vast expanse of the mind,
Blueprints of ideas our fingers find,
Infinite realms intertwined,
Thoughts as delicate as wind-chimed.

Each notion, a crafted stone,
In intellect's edifice, we're not alone,
Wisdom across the ages sown,
Building minds, knowledge known.

Through mortar of doubt and faith's grain,
We construct understanding, disdain pain,
Erecting truth in every lane,
Foundations firm, horizons attain.

Imagination paints the sky,
With the colors thought's wings imply,
In this mental cathedral high,
Unseen dreams will never die.

From silent rooms, ideas leap,
In the heart's core, secrets deep,
Architects of thought, we keep,
Building worlds even as we sleep.

Winged Ideas

In the quiet fold of night,
Ideas take their daring flight,
Winged whispers bathed in light,
Glide through the dark, break the sight.

Caught on breeze, they gently sway,
Emerging with the dawn's first ray,
Dreams that dawn will not allay,
To the light they find their way.

Thoughts turn into vivid schemes,
Worlds unfurl within their dreams,
In the mind's eye, boundless themes,
Infinity in gentle streams.

From feathered whispers life will spring,
In the heart, these hopes take wing,
Memories etched in soft lacing,
Endless skies they now bring.

Soundless flight to find the soul,
Into the universe of whole,
Winged ideas, hearts console,
In us they write their sacred scroll.

Light of Emotions

In shadows, light begins to play,
Emotions rise, they find their way,
From dawn to dusk, a bright display,
Colors of the heart's array.

Expressions soft in twilight's keep,
Tender feelings buried deep,
Awake from their silent sleep,
Across our souls, their light will sweep.

Love's glow in the evening's hue,
A soothing warmth, forever true,
Fear and joy, they intermingle too,
Stars igniting in emotional view.

In every sigh, a spark ignites,
Casting shades in soft delights,
Guiding through the silent nights,
Our hearts become the glowing lights.

Morning breaks with hues anew,
Emotions breathe in skies so blue,
In the light, our spirits grew,
Shining brightly, pure and true.

Visionary Aria

Beyond the hills where dreams reside,
A melody so pure, it glides.
Stars whisper secrets in the night,
Revealing futures bathed in light.

Through veils of time, the visions soar,
In endless skies, they dance and more.
An aria of hope sings clear,
Guiding hearts with no fear.

Each note a wish, each chord a dream,
In the realm where wonders gleam.
Eyes closed, the soul can see,
The world as it was meant to be.

Where shadows fall, they quickly fade,
In this vision, brightly made.
An aria of whispered grace,
Lifts us to a higher place.

The final note, a beacon bright,
Illuminates the endless night.
In the visionary aria, we find,
The boundless beauty of the mind.

Ephemeral Musings

The petals fall with gentle grace,
In silent reverie, they pace.
Moments fleeting, whispers thin,
Life's ephemeral musings begin.

A shadow cast upon the wall,
Echoes of the ages call.
Through the mist, a truth reveals,
In each passing breath, it feels.

The river flows, a silver thread,
Tales untold in waters spread.
Time's tender touch, a soft caress,
In fleeting musings, we confess.

A dream is but a fleeting sigh,
A glimmer in the night's sky.
These musings, brief and sublime,
Fade within the sands of time.

Yet in their wake, a light remains,
Subtle traces, silent gains.
Ephemeral, yet deeply wise,
The musings of our fleeting ties.

Inspired Waveforms

Upon the sea of endless thought,
Waves of insight, gently brought.
Currents weave through dreams and fears,
Drawing close what the heart endears.

Soundless echoes, whispers bright,
Illuminate the boundless night.
Each idea, a crest in time,
In inspired waveforms, so sublime.

The mind, a ship set free to roam,
Through waveforms, it finds its home.
A symphony of light and sound,
Inspiration striking, profound.

Tempests rise, then fade to calm,
In the eye, the soul's sweet psalm.
Each wave a ripple in the sea,
Of boundless creativity.

Anchored not, the journey's true,
Through inspired realms, we view.
Waveforms dancing through the mind,
Infinite, unique, unconfined.

Echoes of the Abstract

In the abstract, colors blend,
Shapes and forms that never end.
A tapestry of thoughts entwined,
In echoes through the vast unlined.

The silence speaks a thousand screams,
Reality is stitched with dreams.
Fragments of the unknown weave,
Patterns in which we believe.

Through the chaos, order finds,
A rhythm in the scattered minds.
Echoes linger, soft and stark,
In the abstract, leaving marks.

A dance of light, a brush of air,
Concepts born with tender care.
In the formless, life takes hold,
Every echo, tales untold.

The abstract world, a canvas wide,
On its surface, truths collide.
Echoes of the thoughts we cast,
In the abstract, they forever last.

The Seraph's Artwork

Beneath celestial skies, where angels tread,
Brushes of light, in twilight's spread.
Stars painted gold, in vast expanse,
Every twinkle, a divine romance.

Petals of dawn in hues so bright,
Whispers of love in shades of light.
Heaven's canvas, pure and white,
With seraph's touch, becomes the night.

Feathers falling, soft and slow,
Creating patterns in moon's glow.
Melodies of silence, soft and sweet,
In artistry, angels their tales repeat.

Mystical hands in graceful sway,
Crafting dreams from realms away.
Infinite beauty carved in light,
The seraph's artwork, night's delight.

Eternal muse in endless flight,
Transforming dark into delight.
Under wings of celestial might,
Art born of stars ignites the night.

Odyssey of Concept

In realms where thoughts dare to dream,
Flows the essence of a cosmic stream.
Ideas weave through time and space,
In the odyssey of mind's embrace.

Whispers of wisdom float on high,
Concepts reaching to touch the sky.
Journeys end where visions start,
In endless quests of the creative heart.

Paradoxes in symphony dance,
Within the universe of chance.
Mystery sings in silent grace,
Through the unseen, concepts trace.

Through valleys deep and heights untold,
Mind's horizons vast and bold.
Every thought a wondrous flight,
In the odyssey of eternal light.

Boundless realms in endless sight,
Where reason meets the infinite night.
Adventures born from every spark,
In journeys of the mind's embark.

Imagination's Dance

Dreams take flight on wings of night,
In realms of wonder, pure delight.
Through shadowed paths and skies of blue,
Imagination dances true.

Whispers of winds in twilight's cheer,
Songs of realms both far and near.
Every step a story told,
In dances of the young and old.

Glimmers of stardust in each twirl,
Secrets of a mystical world.
Patterns woven in moonlit trance,
In the bliss of imagination's dance.

Harmonies in colors bright,
Melodies in silver light.
Every beat a tale anew,
A symphony in every hue.

Infinite stories in each sway,
Night and dream in grand display.
Eternal rhythm of heart's chance,
In timeless realms, imagination's dance.

Whispers of Innovation

In silent echoes, thoughts unfold,
Crafting futures brave and bold.
From whispered dreams to grand creation,
Born from seeds of innovation.

Sparks of genius, unseen, unknown,
Silent whispers, seeds are sown.
New worlds bloom in minds so bright,
Guided by the dawning light.

Through shadowed doubts and darkest night,
Come whispered truths into the light.
Ideas bloom where fears once laid,
In whispered tones, new paths are made.

Winds of change in quiet show,
Innovation's whisper makes it so.
Boundaries fall and visions rise,
In whispers heard beneath the skies.

Silent musings, bold and grand,
Craft a future from wisdom's hand.
In whispers, all creation starts,
Innovation's voice in hopeful hearts.

Visionary Tunes

In shadows cast by moon's soft glow,
Whispers of the night do seek,
Melodies where dreamers go,
Across the skies, the stars they speak.

Harmonies in whispered beams,
A dance of timeless, silent lore,
Softly woven, hidden seams,
Crafting visions, evermore.

Eyes closed tight, the mind's stage bright,
Notes of wonder drift and part,
In this realm of endless flight,
Tunes are born, within the heart.

Silhouette of dreams we trace,
The music of the soul in flight,
Guiding through our inner space,
Till dawn transforms the silent night.

In the hush of twilight's grace,
Visionary tunes do start,
A spectral symphony's embrace,
Crafted in the dreamer's heart.

Crafted Crescendo

Hands composing, crafting lines,
Notes that soar and softly sigh,
Rhythms where the spirit shines,
From fingers, music starts to fly.

Building arches, lifting high,
The melody where feelings grow,
Each crescendo to the sky,
A journey both sublime and slow.

Pulse of passion, steady beat,
Crafted with a knowing hand,
Echoes from the heart's own seat,
A symphony that understands.

Shaping sound as sculptors do,
A crescendo in the mind,
Every note reveals what's true,
Expressions of the heart combined.

From silence to the loudest cheer,
Crafted in the soul's own blend,
Crescendo crafted year by year,
It's music that will never end.

Minds in Motion

Thoughts that dance in endless streams,
Ideas racing, minds in flow,
In the world of crafted dreams,
Where the seeds of wisdom grow.

Wandering through mind's expanse,
Every notion takes its course,
Through the rhythm of the chance,
Guided by an unseen force.

Puzzles forming, then complete,
Patterns shifting, ever bold,
Minds in motion never fleet,
Stories of the future told.

In the search for what could be,
In each mental wave and crest,
We rewrite our destiny,
With each thought, our minds invest.

Yet within this vibrant dance,
Truth in motion reveals all,
With each visionary glance,
In the mind's eternal hall.

The Artist's Pulse

In the heart where visions birth,
Pulses beat with fervent grace,
Canvases of life and earth,
Color dances in the space.

Every stroke a breath of life,
Every hue a tale unfolds,
In the brush, the fleeting strife,
In the hands, the heart's own holds.

Eyes perceive beyond the plain,
Crafting realms of boundless sight,
In the midst of joy and pain,
Art becomes the endless light.

Carving dreams with graphite lead,
Or with oils deep and rich,
In these strokes, the spirits thread,
Every moment, every stitch.

Through the artist's pulsing beat,
Creation's flow finds its place,
In each masterpiece, complete,
Lies the heart's eternal trace.

Wanderlust Dreams

In the whisper of the forest green,
Where rivers sing a gentle theme,
Mountains rise, a serene screen,
In wanderlust, I find my dream.

Fields of gold stretch wide and far,
Underneath the evening star,
With every step, a world bizarre,
My heart's desire, no bizarre.

Shores embraced by crystal waves,
Tales of sailors, restless braves,
In this journey, love engraves,
Echoes of old souls it saves.

City lights, a golden thread,
To distant lands where stories spread,
Adventures live where dreams are fed,
Wanderlust gleams ahead, ahead.

Through valleys deep and peaks so high,
Underneath the open sky,
As time goes swift, my spirit flies,
In wanderlust, dreams never die.

Tales from the Easel

Canvas stretched, a silent plea,
In colors wild, my soul sets free,
Brush in hand, I start to see,
Tales that whisper truth to me.

A stroke of blue, a dash of gold,
Stories of the young and old,
Each hue a battle fierce or cold,
In painted tales, my hand upholds.

Figures dance in shadows light,
In every corner, tales of night,
From dawn to dusk, a painter's flight,
In colors traced, a story's might.

Silent whispers through the air,
Every portrait, memories share,
A world within, tender and rare,
On this easel, dreams declare.

No words are spoken, none are heard,
In every shape, a silent word,
Eternal tales, gently stirred,
Through brush and paint, emotions spurred.

Brushstrokes of Thought

On a blank, untainted space,
Thoughts emerge, traces of grace,
Brushstrokes carve a timeless face,
In this art, mind's labyrinth trace.

Colors blend, from dark to light,
Fleeting glimpses, day to night,
Each stroke holds a piece of sight,
Stories etched in black and white.

Swirls and lines, chaotic peace,
In every curve, thoughts release,
On the canvas, worries cease,
Brushstrokes form, a mind's caprice.

Dreams collide in patterns bold,
Mysteries in hues unfold,
In every inch, a tale retold,
Brushstrokes paint the heart's true gold.

In silence, thoughts take their flight,
As the brush weaves day from night,
Eternal stories brought to light,
In brushstrokes, art and thought unite.

Muses in the Moonlight

Underneath the moon's soft glow,
Muses whisper all they know,
In this light, their voices flow,
In moonlight streams, my thoughts bestow.

Shadows dance in silver beams,
Guiding stars and glowing streams,
Muses weave their haunting dreams,
In moonlit nights, nothing seems.

Poems born from midnight air,
Words so delicate, tender, rare,
In the calm, my soul lays bare,
Muses' whispers everywhere.

Luna's glow, a sacred shrine,
Where muses' voices intertwine,
In their light, my thoughts align,
In moonlit muse, dreams define.

Through the night, till dawn's embrace,
Muses linger, leave no trace,
In moonlight, words interlace,
Eternal whispers time can't erase.

Symphony of Minds

In a realm where thoughts embrace,
Ideas dance in endless chase,
Woven strings of intellect,
Compose a symphony, perfect.

Wisdom flows through every vein,
Whispered truths that break the chains,
Harmony of hearts and mind,
In unity, new paths we find.

Voices merge in subtle chord,
Silent rapture, unseen lord,
Guiding light in twilight's hue,
Boundless wonders, minds renew.

Echoes rise in crescendo,
Majestic peaks, serene below,
Each mind a note in grand rapport,
Together, we transcend the shore.

Infinite, the journey calls,
Bound by thought's cathedral halls,
In this symphony of minds,
Eternity, our fates unwind.

The Muse's Echo

In shadows deep, where dreams reside,
The muse's whispers softly guide,
A spark ignites, a flame anew,
Endless tales come into view.

Through barren lands of muted sound,
Her gentle voice, my thoughts unbound,
In echoes clear, her song does flow,
Painting skies with twilight's glow.

Verses spun from threads of dreams,
Cascading down in silver streams,
A symphony of stars aligned,
In her echo, peace we find.

Secrets sung in ancient rhyme,
Weaving magic, halting time,
A dance of words in silken air,
Through her echo, everywhere.

In her shadowed steps, I tread,
Following her voice ahead,
The muse's echo, deep and true,
Bringing forth the old, the new.

Coloring Thoughts

Brushstrokes light on canvas bare,
Ideas bloom in vibrant flair,
Hues of wisdom, shades of grace,
In every thought, a new embrace.

Palette rich with endless dreams,
Pouring forth in radiant streams,
Each hue a whisper, soft and bright,
Coloring thoughts with pure delight.

Rainbow arcs across the mind,
In luminescent threads entwined,
Creating realms of endless scope,
Where every shade becomes our hope.

Vivid scenes in minds take flight,
Through darkest night to morning light,
Blending memories, joys, and fears,
Coloring thoughts through silent years.

Each thought a burst, a blaze anew,
With every brush, a world we view,
In endless colors, thoughts take form,
A tapestry, both wild and warm.

Timeless Pursuits

In the quest for timeless truth,
We walk the paths of dreamt-of youth,
Steps that thread through ageless sands,
Yearning hearts and reaching hands.

Through the tapestry of night,
Guided by an ancient light,
Celestial maps in endless sky,
Drawing paths where angels sigh.

Wisdom sought in circles wide,
Reflections where the stars confide,
In the dance of moonlit beams,
We chase echoes, finding dreams.

Time spins tales in gentle waves,
Each pursuit, a path that paves,
Roads of wonder, tales untold,
In these pursuits, spirits fold.

Beyond the dawn, the quest remains,
Through sunwashed fields and shadowed lanes,
In these timeless pursuits, we see,
The endless flow of destiny.

The Concept Garden

In twilight's gentle, fading light,
Dreams and thoughts entwine, take flight,
Where seeds of wonder softly fall,
To bloom within the mind's vast hall.

Silent whispers, secrets grow,
In fertile soil, ideas know,
A canvas painted by the breeze,
Where muses wander, hearts appease.

Petals whisper tales untold,
In this sanctuary, bold,
Concepts flourish, wild and free,
In gardens of infinity.

Stars descend in silver streams,
Nourishing the land of dreams,
With every dawn, new vistas born,
In fertile minds, ideas adorn.

Thus we tend this sacred space,
With gentle hands and mindful grace,
For in the garden, pure and grand,
Endless possibilities expand.

Creative Currents

Rivers of thought in ceaseless flow,
Where boundless creativity does grow,
Against the current, visions glide,
A symphony of dreams, worldwide.

Sparkling waves of ingenuity,
A dance of light, fluidity,
In currents deep, ideas surge,
To shores unknown, they soon emerge.

Through channels deep and winding bends,
The journey of creation wends,
On tides of thought, we drift away,
To realms where inspiration plays.

Illuminated by the moon's soft glow,
New worlds from our fingers flow,
In these waters clear and bright,
Every shadow finds its light.

From source to sea, the currents wind,
Paths untraveled, thoughts unlined,
In the ebb and flow of time,
Creativity, so pure, divine.

Ideas in Bloom

In gardens where ideas bloom,
Colors swirl and fragrances loom,
A thought, a spark, a tender seed,
From inspiration, dreams proceed.

Rising from the fertile ground,
Voices of the hopeful sound,
Petals soft as whispered sighs,
Reveal new worlds beyond our eyes.

Each blossom holds a whispered truth,
In the tapestry of youth,
Where minds as one do intertwine,
In ideas broad and so divine.

Sunlight kisses every leaf,
Banishing the shadows, grief,
In the meadow of the mind,
Endless beauty there we find.

As flowers turn their gaze above,
Seeking light, and giving love,
So do we, in constant quest,
To let our spirits be expressed.

Voices of Expression

In echoes of the heart's own beat,
A symphony of life, so sweet,
Each voice a thread of golden light,
Woven in the fabric bright.

Expression flows in colors pure,
In melodies that long endure,
From soul to soul, the stories blend,
A dance where spirit has no end.

In whispered tones or joyous cries,
In every tear and every rise,
The chorus of the human race,
Reflected in each hallowed space.

Across the canvas of the night,
Our voices rise, our dreams take flight,
Echoes of eternity,
In the language of the free.

Thus we sing, and thus we speak,
In moments strong and those so weak,
Voices joining, hearts confess,
In the dance of pure express.

Musing Melodies

Through twilight skies, the notes arise,
With gentle hums, the evening sighs,
The stars compose, a lullaby,
In harmony, the spirits fly.

Moon's soft embrace, adorns the night,
In whispered tones, pure and light,
From distant realms, the echoes sound,
As soulful dreams, are gently found.

A fleeting tune, of time and space,
In rhythmic waves, it finds its place,
With every breeze, the cadence flows,
An ancient song, that forever grows.

Instrumental whispers, tell the tale,
Of secrets kept, in night's soft veil,
The world awash, in serenade,
A musing melody, finely made.

Through chords of time, and strings of fate,
The universe, does resonate,
In silent symphony, hearts align,
To the ageless notes, of the divine.

Enchanted Brushstrokes

With every stroke, a world anew,
On canvas white, hues come through,
A dance of light, and shadows play,
In colors bright, the dreams convey.

From verdant fields, to azure skies,
The artist's hand, does mesmerize,
In fleeting swirls, and bold embrace,
A masterpiece, of form and grace.

Each brush's sweep, a tale unfolds,
Of whispered winds, and days of old,
In pigment deep, the soul imparts,
A vision bright, from tender hearts.

Through palettes wide, the stories stream,
Of rivers wild, and glen serene,
In blending shades, life's essence gleams,
An artful world, beyond the dream.

In every hue, a mystery,
A captured light, eternity,
With gentle hand, the magic spins,
An endless realm, where beauty wins.

Form of Fantasy

In realms where dragons rise and soar,
And golden gates, veil tales of yore,
The mystic lands, where heroes stride,
In forms of fantasy, dreams confide.

A castle's hold, on moonlit highs,
With fairies' wings, that kiss the skies,
An elven song, in forest's shade,
In legend's grace, does magic fade.

The wizard's spell, with staff alight,
In crystal caves, where gems ignite,
The ancient scripts, in tongues unknown,
In whispered chants, the seeds are sown.

Through portals vast, and timeless seas,
The fabled beasts, and sacred trees,
In every word, a saga weaves,
A boundless lore, that mind believes.

The fantasy, a realm so wide,
Where inner worlds, in wonder bide,
In myths and dreams, the heart does see,
A boundless land, where souls are free.

Rhymes of Insight

When dawn unfolds her golden veil,
And morning whispers start to trail,
The world awakens, thoughts ignite,
In rhymes of truth, and pure insight.

Through daily paths, the wisdom flows,
In whispered lines, the spirit grows,
With every turn, and twist of fate,
An insight clear, the soul does sate.

In shadowed depths, or sunlit peaks,
Within the quiet, insight speaks,
Of life's design, in rhythm clear,
The rhymes of insight, we hold dear.

A poet's pen, the truths reveal,
In rhyming words, the wounds can heal,
From ancient tomes, to modern time,
The cycles of, an endless rhyme.

In quiet thought, the answers glide,
Through limpid dreams, where truths abide,
And in the heart, the wisdom lies,
In rhymes of insight, clear as skies.

Crafted Epiphanies

In silence, whispers weave the night,
Musing thoughts take gentle flight,
Crafting dreams from twilight beams,
Epiphanies in shadowed streams.

Stars above, canvas so wide,
Painted hopes in cosmic tide,
Secrets dance in stellar flair,
Wisdom cloaked in midnight's air.

Through the veil of day's disguise,
Hidden truths for seeking eyes,
Crafted hearts and minds so keen,
Chasing visions yet unseen.

Moments pass on timeless wings,
Epiphanies that quiet brings,
Leaves of thought, in autumn's breeze,
Unfold like tales from ancient trees.

Revelations gently bloom,
Petals fall in silent room,
Crafted notions, dreams set free,
In the still of reverie.

Visionary Verse

In the hush of morning's glow,
Whispered winds of futures blow,
Verses carried on the light,
Guiding hearts to broader sight.

Scribes of destiny, pens in hand,
Chart new realms in dreamlike sand,
Imagination's boundless sea,
Crafts the fates for you, for me.

Stars align in cosmic prose,
Night's blanket where wisdom grows,
Tales of wonder, lines so pure,
Mark the paths we must endure.

In visions clear, the poets write,
Words of power, truths in flight,
Verses carve eternal streams,
Flowing through our waking dreams.

Whispers turn to mighty roars,
Visionaries tales, evermore,
In the ink of boundless skies,
Lives the verse where promise lies.

Labors of Muse

From the well of silent thought,
Muse ignites what time has brought,
Whispered words in twilight fade,
Emerging from the dreams we've laid.

Toil in mind's vast, endless plains,
Crafting wonders, shunning chains,
Through the storms and through the night,
Muse inspires the bearer's plight.

Scraps of hope and fragments wild,
By muse's hand are reconciled,
Labors gentle, fierce, and true,
Form the world in varied hue.

Inspiration's whispered breath,
Chases fears of loss and death,
Spun from spirit, toil, and dream,
We find our place in muse's theme.

Every note and every word,
In the heart's core, deeply stirred,
Labors lived with muse combined,
Craft the tales we've yet to find.

Ember of Imagination

From the spark of silent night,
Flickers sparks of endless light,
Imagination's gentle flare,
Illuminates the hidden lair.

In the void where thoughts arise,
Embers glow, igniting skies,
Casting shadows, casting dreams,
Painting life in vibrant themes.

Wandering minds, do dare to leap,
Across the chasms, endless deep,
Ember's light as guide and lore,
Opening each unseen door.

Through the haze of fleeting time,
Burns the heart of muse's chime,
Fusion of the dark and bright,
Crafts the tales within the night.

From ember's glow to roaring blaze,
Imagination's endless maze,
Guides us through the vast unknown,
To worlds where dreams are fully grown.

Wellspring of Ideas

From depths unseen, the thoughts arise,
In dreams and whispers, under starlit skies.
A surge of visions, bold and bright,
Crafting worlds beyond our sight.

Each spark a genesis of new,
Where endless wonders cascade through.
Minds entwine in creativity's dance,
Seizing the moment, seizing the chance.

Rivers of insight, they converge,
In pools of wisdom, thoughts emerge.
An endless cascade, never dry,
An intellectual supply.

From crumbling parchments, wisdom's flow,
Roots of history, seeds we sow.
To heights of innovation climb,
Creating wonders of our time.

In quietude, the fountain lies,
Awaiting seekers, the curious eyes.
Drink deep from this eternal spring,
Where boundless inspiration will always cling.

Sketches in Solitude

In silent rooms, the pencil glides,
Across the paper, secrets hide.
Each stroke a whisper, tales unfold,
In solitude, pure gold.

Figures emerge in shadowed grace,
Contours of dreams dance in space.
Lines entwine in silent song,
Art in solitude, where hearts belong.

Voices mute, yet thoughts speak clear,
In isolation, feelings near.
A world within the painted scene,
In loneliness, the soul is seen.

Canvas white, a void to fill,
With every sketch, time stands still.
Expressions form in gentle hand,
In quiet realms, they understand.

Solitude, a muse profound,
Where purest artistry is found.
Alone, but with a myriad,
In sketches, worlds are born and live.

Labyrinth of Aesthetics

Lost within the curving maze,
Of beauty's spell, in twilight's haze.
Each corner turned, a sight anew,
Each step a brush of different hue.

Winding paths of light and shade,
In this labyrinth, visions laid.
Textures rich, in woven thread,
Through myriad ways, the senses led.

Colors splash in arcs and flow,
In spirals where our fancies go.
Textures sing in silence loud,
Aesthetic dreams, no bounds allowed.

Traverse the winding corridors,
Of elegance and whispered doors.
In every niche a secret lies,
In every glance, new wonder rises.

Thus we wander, hearts alight,
In this labyrinth, day and night.
Through endless twists, we find the core,
The beauty that we all adore.

Melodies of Imagery

In visions clear, the mind song flows,
Melodies of thought in gentle prose.
Each image traced in sounds conceived,
Finding harmony, unperceived.

Frames of moments, captured sweet,
In visual tunes, our hearts they meet.
Symphonies of stills combine,
Crafting dreams within the line.

Colors hum in silent chords,
Through each hue, a note affords.
Resonating in the soul,
Every glimpse, a story told.

Shadows dance in rhythm's grace,
Silent echoes in their place.
Compositions of the mind,
In melody, the sight refined.

Thus we craft with senses all,
Melodies in image fall.
Through eyes, we hear the whispering notes,
In frame and thought, the music floats.

Resonance of Creation

In twilight's embrace, whispers begin,
The cosmos hums, a song within.
Stars ignite tales in the dark,
An artist's soul leaves its mark.

Mountains echo ancient lore,
Oceans sing to a distant shore.
Every heartbeat merges in rhyme,
The universe dances, echoing time.

From roots deep in earth's embrace,
Sprouts life with endless grace.
Winds carry a timeless tune,
Creation's symphony beneath the moon.

Clouds paint on a sky so wide,
Raindrops tap out nature's guide.
In every corner, a story awaits,
The resonance of life permeates.

From dawn's birth to night's deep hue,
Creation breathes, forever new.
With every breath, a new narration,
Whispers the resonance of creation.

Pen's Luminous Edge

Ink flows like rivers on a page,
Words alight, breaking the cage.
Dreams take flight, minds unfurl,
In every phrase, a secret pearl.

Shadows dance beneath the lines,
In hidden depths, clarity shines.
Each letter, a star in the night,
The pen's glow, an endless light.

Sprouting from a writer's core,
Stories and truths freely pour.
A world's edge is shaped anew,
In the ink, both false and true.

Boundless realms in every stroke,
Ideas whispered, gently spoke.
From dawn's rise to twilight's nudge,
Crafted by a pen's luminous edge.

Every end is a fresh start,
Stories stitched in the heart.
With every word, tales woven,
In ink, the spirit's token.

Frames of Revelation

Captured moments in silent frames,
Each image whispers sacred names.
Past and present seamlessly bind,
Clues to the truth we often find.

Shattered glass reveals the whole,
In every shard, a story bold.
Time freezes in a single shot,
A mosaic of every thought.

Blinking through the lens of fate,
Life unfolds at a measured rate.
In shadows, light and truth combine,
Creating visions, deeply divine.

Gazing deep within each scene,
Life's mysteries softly glean.
Every frame a revelation,
A frozen poem of creation.

Moments of joy, scenes of sorrow,
Truths of today, glimpses of tomorrow.
Bound by frames, our fleeting view,
Yet within, revelations that renew.

Vibrations of Vision

Through the haze of morning's kiss,
Nature murmurs tales of bliss.
Trees sway to the silent beat,
Hearts align where visions meet.

Lifting eyes to the heavenly skies,
Stars vibrate with whispered lies.
Moonlight's touch ignites the core,
In the silence, visions soar.

Paths unseen by mortal sight,
Emerge in the velvet night.
Dreams and thoughts crystallize,
Glimpses of truth, so wise.

Rivers carve the silent land,
Guided by an unseen hand.
With every step, there's a way,
In vibrations, visions play.

A canvas vast, the world unfurled,
Messages within every swirl.
In vibrations, the future gleams,
Vision birthed in ethereal streams.

Muse's Embrace

In whispering winds, the muse appears,
A touch of grace that calms all fears,
With gentle hands, she paints the night,
And fills the soul with boundless light.

Oh, tender muse, with eyes so deep,
In silence, secrets do you keep,
You weave the stars into a tale,
Where dreams ascend and troubles pale.

Upon your wings, my heart takes flight,
To realms of wonder, pure delight,
In every note, your magic sings,
A symphony on gossamer strings.

Through time and space, we glide as one,
Beneath the moon, beneath the sun,
A dance of shadows, light, and mist,
In Muse's Embrace, we coexist.

So evermore, within your thrall,
I heed your whispered, far-off call,
For in your arms, my spirit flies,
Bound only by the endless skies.

Crafted Illuminations

In candlelight, the shadows play,
Crafted forms that wind and sway,
Each flicker tells a tale of old,
A story in the flame, retold.

The artisan with careful hand,
Shapes the magic, grains of sand,
From molten glass to life anew,
Illuminations crafted, true.

A glow that pierces darkest night,
With colors vibrant, pure, and bright,
Each spark a dream, a wish, a prayer,
In crafted worlds, they linger there.

Through craft and art, we see the soul,
In flickers, embers, burning coal,
A mirror to the human heart,
In every piece, we find our part.

So light the lamps and let them gleam,
In crafted lights, we dare to dream,
For in their glow, we find our way,
And night is turned to golden day.

Harmonies of Thought

In quiet minds, the thoughts align,
A melody, a perfect line,
With every breath, a note is born,
A symphony from dusk till morn.

Ideas dance in gentle waves,
Their echoes from the heart's deep caves,
Each harmony a story spun,
A dialogue that's just begun.

The chords of wisdom softly play,
In rhapsodies of night and day,
Within the silence, truths are sought,
In woven strands of subtle thought.

Oh, harmonies that shape our view,
In whispered tones, both old and new,
You guide us through the shadowed haze,
To find the light in darkened days.

So let the mind's sweet music flow,
In harmonic whispers, let us grow,
For in the symphony of thought,
Our highest dreams and hopes are caught.

Inspiration's Tapestry

Threads of light and shadow blend,
With every weave, the colors mend,
A tapestry of thought and scheme,
Embroidery of life, a dream.

Through needles sharp and hands so skilled,
Creative visions are fulfilled,
Each pattern tells a tale unique,
In every stitch, our spirits speak.

The canvas vast, yet fibers fine,
In every loop, our stars align,
With hues of warmth, with shades of night,
In woven textures, we find light.

From threads of gold to silver grey,
The stories form, they guide our way,
A patchwork quilt of hopes and fears,
Of laughter's joy, of sorrow's tears.

In Inspiration's Tapestry,
We find the soul's deep majesty,
For every thread and every seam,
Is bound by love and crafted dream.

Ink and Idea

Within the quiet of my mind,
Words on paper, echoes bind.
Ink flows like a river's gleam,
Building bridges to a dream.

Inspiration whispers through the air,
Crafting tales without a care.
Each line a step, a soul's decree,
A voyage in creativity.

Colors merge in twilight hues,
Ideas sprout, like morning's dews.
Every verse a world to see,
Bound in ink, eternally.

Wisdom danced in written form,
In a tempest calm and warm.
Eyes trace paths on thoughts' terrain,
Ink and idea, vast domain.

Every story, every rhyme,
Transcends the boundaries of time.
In the silent, secret night,
Ink and idea take their flight.

Sculpted Musings

Chisel strikes the marble stone,
Shapes unknown, thoughts alone.
Art emerges from the guise,
Dreams to life, they crystallize.

Silent whispers, form anew,
Figures dance within the view.
Granite breathes through hands so skilled,
Sculpted musings, will fulfilled.

Stone and spirit, meld as one,
Crafting wonders, never done.
In the rhythm of the craft,
Time and essence intertwine and draft.

Figures born from silent clay,
Speak a language none betray.
In their gaze, the stories told,
Of the musings etched in bold.

Silent hands revive the past,
Shaping forms that ever last.
In each line and curve, the soul,
Sculpted musings make us whole.

Dreamweaver's Symphony

Strings of starlight, notes of night,
Composing dreams in pure delight.
Melodies of moonbeams flow,
In a symphony that seems to glow.

Harps of hope, with chords so fine,
Crafting songs of the divine.
Each refrain a drift through sky,
Dreams set free to never die.

Harmonies of whispered air,
Brush against the heartstrings bare.
Conductor of the twilight's blend,
Dreamweaver's tunes that never end.

Echoes form in silent streams,
Orchestrating boundless dreams.
In each measure, soft and free,
Flows the dreamweaver's symphony.

Ephemeral the notes exist,
In a realm of gentle mist.
Every dream a melody,
In the eternal symphony.

Thoughts Unfurled

In the silence of the dawn,
Thoughts like blooms on canvas drawn.
Mind's garden, ever bright,
In the whispering morning light.

Ideas blossom into prose,
Petals soft in intricate rows.
Every thought a rare design,
Crafted in the heart's confine.

Sunlight dances on each line,
Warming words in pure divine.
As the morning's beams unfurl,
Thoughts emerge and softly swirl.

In the breeze, they learn to fly,
Stories, secrets, reaching sky.
Every notion, each new world,
In the daybreak, thoughts unfurled.

Wisps of wonder, cloudless blue,
Form the dreams that once we knew.
In this dawn so free, so pearled,
Lie our deepest thoughts, unfurled.

Beacons of Ingenuity

In shadows cast by doubt and fear,
We forge ahead, a path to clear.
With minds aligned, in unity,
They shine as beacons, ingenuity.

The night may fall, the winds may howl,
Yet through the storm, we still endow.
With visions bold and hearts sincere,
Create anew, we hold so dear.

In realms of thought, where dreams ignite,
We chase the dawn, dispel the night.
Through trials vast and doubts profound,
Our spirit's strength will know no bound.

From sparks to flames, ideas arise,
A symphony 'neath boundless skies.
They rally forth, a guiding star,
In even dark, they wander far.

To futures bright, our journey flows,
With endless hope, our courage grows.
Together, minds in harmony,
We build tomorrow, endlessly.

Pianist's Inner Fire

Hands that dance on ivories white,
Crafting worlds in day and night.
Each key a tale, a whisper soft,
In melody, our souls aloft.

The notes cascade, a river's sweep,
In minor chords, our secrets keep.
With every stroke, a fire ignites,
Composing dreams in starry nights.

A tempest fierce, then silence still,
The pianist's touch, a guiding will.
From sorrow's depths to joy's embrace,
In every sound, a truth we trace.

Eternal flames within them burn,
Through time and space, our hearts they turn.
Their fingers swift, emotions bared,
A symphony by passion paired.

Beyond the world of strings and wood,
Their language echoes, understood.
In every pulse, desire's choir,
We hear the pianist's inner fire.

Gales of Innovation

Upon the winds of change we ride,
Through unknown lands, horizons wide.
With minds unbound, we chase the storm,
A new frontier our spirits form.

In whispers soft, ideas crest,
Among the gales, our thoughts invest.
Where others cease, we venture far,
Our guiding light, a curious star.

Innovation, bold and fierce,
Its gales through clouds of doubt do pierce.
We sculpt the winds, their force we tame,
And blaze a trail in freedom's name.

Each breeze a spark, a novel dawn,
In every whisper, futures spawn.
Through trials harsh, we still aspire,
To fan the gales, our hearts require.

Collaborate with nature's force,
On gales of change, we set our course.
In every gust, a chance anew,
To build a world, both bright and true.

Sculptor's Secret

In the marble's silent plea,
A form of grace, a mystery.
The sculptor's hand, with vision clear,
Unveils the truth that lies so near.

Each chiselled stroke, a breath of life,
Through stone and dust, the artist's strife.
With gentle touch, the secrets yield,
A figure's soul, at last revealed.

From rugged block to polished gleam,
The sculptor weaves a timeless dream.
In every curve, a tale untold,
Through hands of art, the stone unfolds.

The whispers soft of hidden muse,
In silence deep, the sculptor's clues.
They carve away the world unseen,
To free the form, both pure and keen.

In every statue, locked within,
The sculptor's secret, truths begin.
They shape and mold the hard facade,
To share with us the mind of god.

Voices of Vision

In twilight beams the whispers call,
From shadowed glades where spirits sprawl.
They sing through mists, both near and far,
Guiding hearts by their gentle star.

Old echoes vie in silent streams,
Bridging worlds through moonlit dreams.
Each soul's tale, a vibrant hue,
In the tapestry of dawn's soft blue.

Through time's corridors they glide,
Unseen bonds that mystics ride.
Ancient lore and futures bright,
Entwined in whispers of the night.

The watcher's eye, the poet's pen,
Chart the realms unseen by men.
In realms of thought, they take their flight,
Crafting worlds in purest light.

By secret paths, in hidden glades,
Voices rise from silent shades.
Their chorus builds, unseen, unheard,
A symphony in every word.

Dreams Painted Anew

On canvas vast, night's dreams unfold,
Whispers in hues both brave and bold.
A touch of gold, a streak of blue,
Worlds reborn in colors true.

Brush in hand, the dreamer wakes,
To dance in dawn's first gentle breaks.
Each starlit spark, a tale unspun,
Awaiting light of morning sun.

In every sweep, a wish, a prayer,
To mend hearts laid cold and bare.
Hope renewed in shades of grace,
Found in night's serene embrace.

Lines that twist in whimsical ways,
Speak of hearts through timeless days.
Each stroke a path, each hue a gate,
To realms beyond night's dreaming state.

As dawn ascends, the colors fade,
But dreams remain in twilight made.
In shadows cast, a promise true,
Of worlds within, forever new.

Soul's Craft

From silent depths the muse will rise,
To cast its spell through darkened skies.
In shadows deep, it weaves its art,
Stitching dreams from heart to heart.

Each woven thread, a whisper's song,
Binding old to new, the weak to strong.
In looms of fate, the craft unfolds,
Mysteries of the soul it holds.

With gentle hand and patient care,
It mends the fabric worn and bare.
The tapestry of life resumes,
In every thread, a thousand blooms.

Beyond the veil where spirits fly,
The silent weaver's hands apply,
A touch of grace, a hint of light,
To guide us through the darkest night.

Its masterwork, unseen yet known,
In every heart, its seeds are sown.
In life's great loom, we find our part,
In the endless weave of soul's art.

The Inventive Beat

A rhythm pulsed in beats unknown,
A heart that dances on its own.
From chaos bright, a tune evolves,
Inventive beats in night dissolves.

In streets alive with hum and haste,
Imagination finds its taste.
Each step, a note, a whispered plea,
To craft the world in harmony.

The dreamer's stride, in sync with stars,
Charts new paths from here to Mars.
In every move, a story wends,
Through twists of time, it never ends.

Drumbeats rise in echoing halls,
In every note, a spirit calls.
To build, to break, to bend anew,
The rhythm's path, both bold and true.

By day or night, the cadence flows,
In lives entwined, the music grows.
The beat invents, it dreams, it flies,
In every heart, the rhythm lies.

Heart's Blueprint

In the chambers softly dark,
Emotions draw their chart,
With every beat and every spark,
An artful, mapped-out heart.

Its pathways thread with care,
Each moment etched in line,
A love's intricate affair,
In patterns so divine.

Through joy and sorrows deep,
A tapestry of soul,
A blueprint that we keep,
Makes everything feel whole.

With passion's ink we trace,
The contours of our dreams,
In every hidden place,
Where light of feeling gleams.

So let the heart unfold,
Its atlas rich and vast,
In stories it has told,
And futures yet to cast.

Artful Rhythms

In the cadence of the night,
A symphony takes flight,
Breathing life in every note,
A melody we wrote.

With each strum and beat,
Emotions find their feet,
Dancing on the waves of sound,
Where our spirits are unbound.

Colors painted with a tune,
Underneath a silver moon,
Artful rhythms in the air,
Music weaving everywhere.

Echoes of our hopes and fears,
In harmonies we hold dear,
Every chord a silent cheer,
A whisper we can hear.

So let us string along,
The melodies so strong,
In every heartbeat song,
We forever do belong.

Inspired Patterns

Woven threads in ancient lore,
Patterns rich and pure,
Each design an open door,
To truths that we endure.

In the fabric of the past,
Stories interlace,
Every stitch a spell is cast,
In time's own tender space.

Geometry of thought,
Shapes in shadows wane,
In lines that we have sought,
Our dreams we shall sustain.

Symmetry in love and loss,
A balance brave and bright,
In patterns we emboss,
The day turns into night.

Inspired by the infinite,
In every fragile thread,
Patterns rise and subtly sit,
On paths where we have tread.

Canvas of Consciousness

In dreams we paint the scenes,
Of realms we've never seen,
A canvas of the mind,
Where endless thoughts align.

Colors blend and mix,
In strokes both bold and light,
A consciousness affixed,
On the spectrum of the night.

Imagination roams,
Through valleys rich and wild,
On canvas it becomes,
Manifest and reconciled.

Shapes that twist and turn,
In patterns deep and vast,
On this canvas we discern,
The future from the past.

Each moment is a hue,
On consciousness bestowed,
In every breath, anew,
We paint the life we've sowed.

Milton Keynes UK
Ingram Content Group UK Ltd.
UKHW020633010824
446326UK00013B/320

9 789916 862735